# Fall Awake

# Fall Awake

Jeannie Wallace McKeown

Published in 2020 by Modjaji Books

Cape Town, South Africa

www.modjajibooks.co.za

© Jeannie Wallace McKeown

Jeannie Wallace McKeown has asserted her right
to be identified as the author of this work.

Edited by Megan Hall

Cover text and artwork by Roxanne Schoon

Book layout by Andy Thesen

Set in Minion Pro


ISBN print: 978-1-928433-00-2

e-book   978-1-928433-01-9

For Wendy and Neil Wallace, who loved my
poetry and always encouraged me to write.
I miss you both terribly.

# Contents

# Boots

Those boots –
the ones I didn't buy in 92
but wanted to
*oh* so much:
red oxblood 8 eye
shit-kicking boots,
*bovver* boots,
whether worn with jeans or dresses
all eyes would be
on the boots,
shone with wax,
*don't-fuck-with-me* boots,
*I'm a lesbian* boots.

I didn't buy them,
only half a lesbian
then and now;
didn't kick up much shit
in my timid twenties.

Now there are the boots
on a website;
*Don't-fuck-with-me.*
I want them still.

# Waiting

I was ten
and she was playing Snow White
in the school play,
singing solo
*someday my prince will come.*

She left me unable to breathe,
craving a different element
to stay alive:
her attention, her smile.
In each performance I sang
only for her.
If there was an audience,
I don't remember.

Only her dark hair,
only her blue eyes,
her voice,
waiting for a prince.

# Confession

Once I laughingly confessed
to the desire to taste you,
to lick a delicate line
across your salted-caramel skin,
the colour of days spent walking to campus
in bare-armed summer dresses,
supine afternoons in the Botanical Gardens
as the light slipped sideways off your shoulders
towards evening.

## Startle

Never again a man,
I thought; I believed
in only the slim, agile fingers
of other women
inside and around me,
polished skin, breasts,
nipples pebbled for sucking

but your angular hands,
calloused fingerpads plucking
the six strings, the guitar's
deep notes carrying
your voice across the grass,
set shooting stars alight
in my belly,
sparking lower
and lower

startling me.

# Seduced

In the narrow side street
by the restaurant's door
you pressed me against
your Golf's steelchrome heat,
kissed me
with bristles and tongue.

You ordered red wine in a jug,
coiled its dark plum flavour
around your mouth;
I wanted to take it from you
with my own.

What did we talk about? I don't recall.
I remember laughing,
and later,
kissing again
in the wine-sweet dark.

## Outside the Youth Hostel

Decanted from the train,
everything I own on my back,
4 pm January late-sun
post-Christmas lights and sales,
*peoplepeoplepeople*
I raise my hand
to the youth hostel bell;
I'm a new photo
on a London Travelcard,
girl in a pink jersey
first-time-on coat.

# First English Winter

Mornings in Wembley,
snow thick around the bus shelter.

A hot climate seedling,
out of place and out of season,
I would leave the house
with newly washed hair.

For a week of mornings
my hair froze,
and I snapped it,
strand by strand
into a fringe,
uneven, jagged blonde ends,
like dropped spaghetti
gathered back carelessly
into the packet.

## Lunch Hour Planes

I took my lunch an hour early.
I wanted new shirts,
so I went to Marks & Spencer's at noon.

No-one looked at anyone else,
not on the street,
not on the long escalator.

The choice was limited. M&S had only winter stock –
they hadn't planned for an Indian summer.
We sweltered in winter shirts and jackets.

It was too hot to eat.
I bought an ice-cold fruit juice,
stopped outside to drink it.

Then I walked back to my office,
across the road from the first Bedlam Hospital,
remembered with a little plaque on the wall.

I was just back,
taking out my new shirts
to show my boss,
when the computer guy
came in and said he
was setting up a TV.

The reception
in our basement office
was pretty poor,
but we saw enough.

The phones kept ringing.
Rumours mostly,
that London was next,
our cataclysm
delayed
only by hours.

The City emptied,
an orderly evacuation.
We watched each other leaving
and when a Boeing 747
disappeared in flight
behind the NatWest Tower

we all stopped,
shared three heartbeats

and when it re-appeared
we said aloud:
*Thank God*
the planes,
the flames,
the tumbling bodies,
burning in our eyes.

# Transformed

Here beside you
I learn your
secret language,
half-breath gasps,
silk of skin, your
flesh leaping
to my touch.

## Seasons

I know before the blood comes
every month,
the summer-heavy ache
in my breasts,
the same every 28 days
since I was eleven;
autumnal blood on toilet paper,
flushed away.

My egg and his sperm,
given every opportunity
to meet,
have not bonded.

Month after month,
each week a season –
my body, remorseless,
will not be breached.
I've failed again
to bring the spring.

## Good News

In the bath, my fuller breasts,
veins stormcloud blue,
alert me to your presence.

I think: perhaps
I will keep you
my secret, for a little while,

but I cannot contain it –
by evening, everyone I know
knows you're coming at last.

# Arrival

After the birth I didn't
feel like a mother, more
a torn, limping creature,
crudely stitched up at the core,
floundering,
breaching depths to snatch
shallow breaths.

My house didn't fit me,
its floors didn't welcome
my steps as I walked
up and down
down and up.
You couldn't suckle,
you screamed,
yellowed like old parchment.

The trip to the hospital,
too fast in the car,
you – panting, tiny, yellow,
incubator
tubes
green room.

My hands,
larger than you,
crept through the portholes
of the glass aquarium,
stroked your head, your feet,
rested on your tentative skin;
your fingers gripped mine.
We held on,
you and I.

# Boyhood

Engrossed in your game
you stand,
shoulder to shoulder,
unaware of my gaze

and I fall awake,
see clearly that you
are no longer babies,
nor even toddlers.
My eyes trace the men
you will grow to be,
strength already mapped
on your bodies.

For now you still creep
into my bed at night,
your small bodies fitting
into the curves and hollows of mine
closer than a lover ever has.

## Takeaway for One

I passed a couple
loitering in the late dusk,
touching hands;
they looked
like the you and me
of five years ago.

The kung po prawns
in the deep fryer
smell as good
as they did
when we ate them,
hot from the packet,
blowing on our fingers.

Paper bag in hand,
my dim reflection
in locked-up shop windows
is my only company
on the short walk home.

# Damage

By the time
I remember
I am self-sufficient

and that your approval
is not the rock
I base my life on anymore,

your careless words
have flayed my heart
open.

## Separated

The kids are asleep.
We made love
the way parents do,
quietly.

They didn't wake,
were already asleep when
you brought them home to me
from their home with you.

Into the curve of your neck I say,
"I still think we could make it."

I feel your shiver; it's cold outside.
Your car starts first time,
reverse lights glowing briefly red,
in warning.

# Rings

You take yours off first;
its absence hits me,
leaving a round
in my chest.

My parents are there.
"Arsehole," my father whispers.
I'm bewildered.
I believed in our promises.

Mine I take off later,
hide it in a box
in the bathroom cabinet.

For months I tap that finger
against the steering wheel,
wondering why
it doesn't chime.

# Ripping

Around the time
my marriage failed
mind and body separated
(tattered torn tenuous)
burnt to bone
wrapped in grey

now

a threadbare patchwork
woven without a loom
has no shape to define
(touch caress hold)
delicately interconnected fragments
remember the ache where a body once was.

# Lawyer's Rooms

"Where is the man I knew,
the one who loved me?"
but you shake me aside,
a stranger,
a bitter one.
A shawl of ice settles over me,
standing beside a ghost,
your doppelganger,
signing papers to cut yourself free.

# Fury

Anger stalks my nights
like a vengeful Fury.

In daylight I repudiate her,
banish her to secret corners,
the barbed-wire traps of my mind.

Shadow to my conscious self,
she hides in wait
for the defenceless dark.

# The Killing Jar

I tell people:
I'm dragonfly-wing thin.

Cobweb-light, I hardly know
where I am
in the expanse I occupy.
They say:
You need to take
better care of yourself.

When they see me laughing
they are satisfied.
There are things I don't say.
I don't say:
hey, this happiness
is scratchcardgold fine.
Scrape a fingernail across it
and it blows away,
sad little curls in a powerful surge

and I fall
into the drowning pool,
the panic lake,
Virginia Woolf's river,
the ocean of Ingrid Jonker.

I fear the next fall
might have no water
to delay me.
I fear the next fall
might be into emptiness,
oxygen replaced by ethyl acetate,
a fall into the killing jar.

# Closing Time

Arriving home, I park,
watch the day fade
pinker and pinker.
The light above the door
flickers on:
inside the emptiness grows.
No-one to put on a light,
turn on the kettle,
hold back the jeering dark.

## Ragged Edge

Growling trucks char the tar outside.
I taste its bitter burning through the air vents.
Inside the car, a radio comedy
pumps voices and canned laughter.
James pops his lips,
hums notes in colour;
copper-flavoured explosions
erupt from his games console.
Nicholas calls from the back seat
*Mommy, Mommy look*
*look at this Mommy.*
I pull hard left to avoid
another truck, hit gravel;
the verge reacts angrily
spits me,
wheels spinning,
back onto the road.

# Dating Website

On the dating website
I write that I love my children.
I laugh less than I would like.
I cry about as much
as every woman.
Under Additional Comments
I write that I didn't end up
where the fairy tales promised,
but fairy tales are unforgiving.
No matter how handsome the prince,
how big the ever after,
I don't believe I would be happy
living in one.

## Possibly a Date

I shave my legs.
It's been winter
and the razor blunts quickly,
drags against my armpit's sagging skin
when I turn my attention there.

I use more soap than usual.
A usual shower takes
five rushed minutes.
Today I'm in there for fifteen;
the water pebbles my skin
before I am done.

The mere hint
that this evening
might be a date
brings iron adrenalin
twanging behind my teeth.

I change the sheets on my bed,
do the washing up.
I breathe deeply,
talk my middle-aged self
out of it every hour.

At 7 pm I leave the house,
still not sure
what this is.

# Higgs Boson

Sitting face to face
across the narrow table,
I made small heaps
from candle drippings,
and shreds of a paper napkin;
you created a swan
from that comedian's flyer.

Our fingers nearly
touched
as we talked,
in the candlelight.

The announcement said
the Higgs Boson had been proven
to exist.
String theory and multiple universes.
I wonder if there was one
where I
touched your hand?

## It's complicated

Some embrace alcohol
to bump over inhibitions
and ask directly
for what they want.

I didn't drink enough
last night,
woke up today
in a bed where you weren't.

## Naked

You'll not be satisfied with the usual things:
flowers, a moon rising, flickering candlelight;
no, you want the bone and the muscle,
you want me to peel back layers
of my needs,
which can only end with me, whispering,

*let me*
*let me please*
kneel to taste that soft, salty skin,
hands to the brown backs of your knees,
explore, with fingers and tongue,
flavours, curves, folds.

## Love Letters

I've woken up needing to write you love letters
saying old-fashioned, sentimental things:
*I am a jug half-empty on a shared table;*
*I am wracked and aching as if with fever*

all of which means, quite simply,
that although you haven't yet left,
your tickets, booked and confirmed,
remind me that the world is a vast place
in which to lose someone.

## Sex After 40

A vibrator doesn't mind if,
on cold nights,
you have sex
with your socks on.

## Stargazing

On a new moon night
my sons ask to stargaze;
we lie on a blanket on the grass.
"Hey," calls James,
"I can see the Southern Cross,
and that dude's belt."

"Orion's," I answer.
"Look, that cloud is a dragon
flying across the moon."
It breathes out cloudy fire;
Nicholas sings "I see it! I saw it straightaway!"

Across the span of the sky
a shooting star flares;
we catch our breath
while it flames and dies.

# Galaxies

James calls me to come see –
"Mommy, hurry up!" – and I,
in a towel, running late,
bite back impatience,
find him, absorbed,
in the sunbeam spanning our kitchen.

He is watching dust motes,
tiny prisms dancing in light.
"Look," his voice is hushed,
"look, it's like galaxies."

Holding his hand, I see through his eyes
systems of stars
a universe wide,
orbiting my shower-wet hair.

# Hijacked

Nicholas laughs at my grimace.
"It's only a toy," he says,
turns it so that I can see
the empty plastic shell
into which bullets are imagined.

In his soft, boy hands
it casts callused shadows,
a snubbed barrel
through the car window
*get out!*

"I don't like guns," I say.

# Notebook

Buried for months
at the bottom
of my everyday bag,
among old sunglasses,
sweets from restaurants,
till slips for groceries
I don't remember eating.

Between the covers I find
snatches of unremembered poems,
in last year's handwriting.

# Writer's Block

I have writer's block
I have writer's block
I have writer's block

I'm sitting in a coffee shop.
I got the table with the comfy sofa.
My coffee is hot because the waiter
brought me hot milk, even though
I asked for cold.
I'm on holiday and I didn't feel like arguing
on the first day of my holiday.
So I poured in the hot milk.
The coffee is bitter.
One spoon of sugar has made no difference.
I can taste the sugar layered over the bitterness,
but it is still there.
I revel in it.
I have a headache.
The coffee is bitter like medicine.

I have writer's block
I have writer's block

There are blonde women here.
These women are glamorous.
I am in a corner
at the table with the comfy sofa,
sipping coffee with one sugar
and my writer's block
and my belly which shows when I lean back,
and my hair which is silvering.
While I sip my bitter coffee

my ex-husband is driving our children
and his parents
along the coastal road on a journey towards me
in this little town.

I have writer's block
I have writer's block

Nothing has happened yet to write about.
Everything is on a knife's edge of nothing happening,
while he drives along the coastal road
and I wait and sip and wait.
The coffee shop sells crafts and arts.
Kitsch but I like them.
Beside the sofa four mannequin legs
stretch flatfooted, toes at my earlobe,
plastered and painted in printed paper,
all in the blues.
The radio plays music from the 60s.

Many people have sat on this sofa before me.
My arse slots into the dip they have left.
My arse.
My comfortable arse
with writer's block
while I sip bitter coffee.
My belly trembles so I suck it in.
The blondes have no bellies
and no arses, but people with arses
have sat on this sofa before,
left their mark.

The waiter tries to take my plate.
I am staring out the window, fork in my hand.
I have eater's block.

This is unusual (see belly, see arse).
My eyes are not seeing the blown tree
or the Coca Cola umbrellas outside.
They are watching the sea on the left
of the car, the traffic on the road,
the wind turbines under which my ex-husband
is driving, with our children and his parents.
I reclaim my plate.
How much easier to resolve eater's block
than writer's block.

I have writer's block
I have writer's block

His parents and my parents have not been together
in four years,
since we split.
This visit is a big deal.
He is bringing them down the coastal road
to my parents' house.
I am not a young woman.
I am not glamorous.
I am not blonde.
My belly shows when I lean back.
My hair is silvering.
I sip bitter coffee on a knife edge in a coffee shop.

Four years since our parents were together.
"You're so lucky," says Jane
(all the artwork is signed *Jane.* Her eyes
are the cobalt blue of the sea.)
"Divorcing and losing family is hard
but you've kept that friendship."
"Yes, yes, we've worked at it,"
I tell her.

I close my eyes, picture the road,
put myself in the car.
"We've worked hard at it,"
I tell my ex-husband at the wheel.
He turns and smiles,
"We'll be there soon."

I drain the last of my coffee.
I embrace my writer's block,
and my bacon and scrambled eggs.
The blondes have all left.
Two women hold hands over the other table
with comfy sofas.
My ex-husband is driving our children
and his parents down the coastal road.
I am right here;
in the dip in the sofa,
belly and silver hair,
sipping bitter coffee.

## All the World

Hours spent dreaming
myself a role
in an infinite
movie reel of lives;
somewhere I moved again
to a faraway country,
somewhere I kissed a girl
before a boy,
somewhere I took a different degree
and am still married, but to someone else,
or to no-one at all.
In some I'm a passenger,
in some I'm the driver of every car I'll ever own.
In some lives I'm thinner;
in others fatter/tireder/more driven/less ambitious.
Some lives I smile more,
some less,
smile cautiously
because this *me* took risks,
smile defiantly
because I took risks,
smile triumphantly
because I am who I want to be.

# Hats

Oh goodness,
someone said,
I didn't realise
you were,
you know.
Bisexual? I said.
Veering to gay,
my girlfriend said.
Lesbian, I agreed.
Yes, *that*,
someone said,
and I thought
I want there to be
some sign
in how I dress
or wear shoes,
a clue
to tip people off
that I,
with kids, a dog,
an average life
can be *that*.
So I went online,
looked up lesbian chic
and gay tattoos
and shoes,
and learnt I should
be wearing hats,
the edgy kind.
It was all
a bit bewildering.
My girlfriend laughed.

I think, she said,
that *that* is all
about how you look
at someone,
hold their gaze.
There's the clue.
So I looked,
and looked
and knew
I'm definitely *that*
with this woman,
and a hat
isn't necessary
after all.

# Acknowledgements

Poems included in this collection have been previously published in the following journals and anthologies:

"Boots", "Confession" and "Galaxies" in *New Coin*; "First English Winter" in *New Contrast*; "All the World" and "Writer's Block" in *Itch*; "Ragged Edge" (published as "Over-stimulated") and "Closing Time" (published as "Returning Home") in *Aerodrome*; "Boyhood", "Possibly a Date", "Sex After 40" and "It's Complicated" in *Aerial*; "Dating Website", "Possibly a Date" and "Sex After 40" (published as "Guilty Pleasure") in *The Looking Glass Anthology* (independently published by Poetree and Jowhari Trahan, 2019), "Higgs Boson" in *Voices of this Land: An Anthology of South African Poetry in English* (Van Schaik, 2017), "Arrival" (published as "Early Arrival") on the AVBOB Poetry Project website (2017).

Printed in the United States
By Bookmasters